pocket: *adjective:* small enough to be carried in the pocket
~~**issue:** *noun:* a vital or unsettled matter~~

Born from a frustration with today's sound-bite driven "rolling" news, Pocket Issue titles pull together the background to some of the biggest challenges facing our world – delivering the facts in an independent and quick-to-digest format.

Designed for our time-pressed lives, these short and pithy handbooks brief you on the big global issues in as little as 20 minutes, giving you the confidence to join the debate.

Praise for Pocket Issue:

'A brilliant wheeze: The essence of the debate in a very approachable format.' Harriet Lane, The Observer

'Exactly what any busy person needs – the facts at your fingertips! Never get caught out again when a conversation starts on the big issues of our time.' Jeremy Vine, BBC Radio 2 & Panorama

'For everyone who longs to be well-informed but lacks the time (or attention span).' Alex Clark, The Observer

'Prep yourself by keeping the one on global warming in the downstairs loo...' Mary Killen, The Spectator

Sign up for news of forthcoming publications and special offers at www.**pocket**issue.com. We always welcome your suggestions and comments.

Pocket issue
Small briefs for a big world

Pocket Issue
Middle East Conflict

Published by Pocket Issue, London
www.**pocket**issue.com
info@**pocket**issue.com

Copyright © Pocket Issue, 2007

ISBN: 0-9554415-2-8
ISBN: 978-0-9554415-2-3

Design by Sanchez Design.
www.sanchezdesign.co.uk

Production by Perfect World Communications.
www.perfectworld.biz

Pocket
issue

Each Pocket Issue is written to a standard editorial template. For Middle East Conflict we'd like to thank the following team:

Research: Was Yaqoob
Writing: Nat Price
Illustration: Andrzej Krauze
Design: Daniel Sanchez, Joandi Schellingerhout
Editorial: Natasha Kirwan, Emma Hardcastle
Advice: Tom Everett Heath

We would also like to thank those who have offered help and advice along the way: Robert Trevelyan, Victoria Dean, Victoria Lane, Mary Alexander, Nick Band, Helen Noel, Dr Jonathan Parry.

The Pocket Issue Team

Contents

Contents

One Minute Guide

The issues in the blink of an eye

ONE MINUTE GUIDE

Key conflict
Middle East, European and American politics have been shaped by a conflict between Israel and the Arab world that stretches back nearly sixty years to 1948, the year Israel was founded.

Palestinian woes
At the core of the conflict is the ongoing discord between Israel and the Palestinian people. This, too, began in 1948 but Jews and Arabs had been fighting in the region since the end of the 19th century.

West meets East
The Cold War brought the West into Middle East politics, though the region's importance to the Christian and Jewish faiths and the rich oil and gas reserves that exist there had captured its attention before then.

Key date – 1948
The year Israel was founded and the start of the first Arab-Israeli war. Over 700,000 Palestinians became refugees in the wake of Israel's victory.

Key date – 1967
The 1967 (Six Day) War between Israel and Arab nations saw Israel occupy the Gaza Strip, the West Bank and East Jerusalem – the territories at the centre of the dispute today.

Peace initiatives
The high-water mark for Israel-Palestinian relations were the 1993 Oslo Accords when a "two-state" solution – Israel and a Palestinian nation living side-by-side – was tabled. Oslo stumbled and the current initiative, the 2002 Roadmap for Peace, appears in tatters.

What they want

The Palestinians want their own state based in the Gaza Strip and the West Bank. Israel wants to secure its borders. Both want East Jerusalem. The wider Arab world wants "justice" for the Palestinians.

Obstacles to peace?

Four main obstacles exist: Jewish settlements in the Occupied Territories. A fair deal for the Palestinians who lost their homes in 1948 and 1967. Sovereignty of Jerusalem. Finally, where the borders should be drawn in a two-state solution.

Standing outside

Islamist militant groups and some Middle Eastern nations refuse to recognise Israel's right to exist. This includes Hamas in the Palestinian territories, Hezbollah in Lebanon, Iran and Syria.

Tensions eased

Forty years ago Israel and the Arab world were locked in conflict. Now many Arab nations are reconciled to Israel's place in the region.

Bleak prospects?

Israel and the Palestinians are fighting. Palestinians and Palestinians are fighting, as are Israel and Hezbollah. The West is entangled in the region.

Peace broker?

The key player in finding a lasting solution will be the USA. Without American involvement it is unlikely that a route to peace can be found.

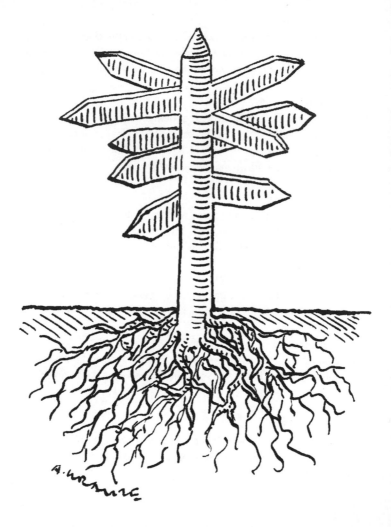

Roots

The important questions answered

MIDDLE EAST CONFLICT – INTRODUCTION

Conflict in the Middle East is never far away from our news bulletins with reports of suicide bombers, rocket attacks, Israeli air strikes and stalling peace initiatives. Even Tony Blair has now taken on the role of a Middle East peace envoy. But what is he trying to resolve? Is a solution possible? And why do events nearly 4,000 miles away matter to us in the UK?

What are the flashpoints in the Middle East?

The ongoing conflict between Israel and the Palestinians that forms the centrepiece of a wider dispute between Israel and the Arab world. More recently, Iraq, and its descent into near civil war since the US-led invasion of 2003, has introduced a new focus for Middle East tension.

This *Pocket Issue* looks at the Arab-Israeli conflict and its impact on the region and the wider world. For a more detailed look at Iraq see **Pocket Issue,** *The War on Terror.*

The Middle East

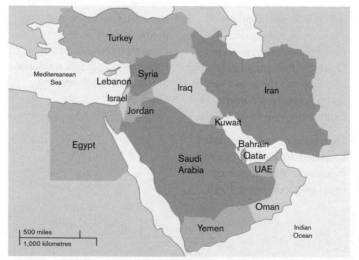

Where is the Middle East?
There is no one clear definition, especially given that the Arab world stretches across North Africa. However, many observers focus on an area bordered by Turkey in the north and Yemen in the south, and by Egypt in the west and Iran in the east.

Why does the Arab-Israeli conflict matter to the UK?
As imperial powers, the UK and other Western nations have been involved in the area since the start of the 20th century, with the UK playing a major role in the origins of the conflict. The Cold War and the struggle with the Soviet Union for influence in the region entrenched this involvement. Currently, the spread of Islamist militancy and the area's rich oil and gas reserves continue to capture the West's attention.

On a human level, the conflict has killed, injured and displaced thousands of people since Israel was founded in 1948.

WHAT IS THE ARAB-ISRAELI CONFLICT?

When did the conflict between Israel and the Arab world begin?
In 1948, the year in which Israel was founded (see *A brief history*). Almost immediately, the surrounding Arab nations attacked the new Israeli state. However, friction between Jewish immigrants and the native Arab population had been sparking in Palestine for several decades prior to 1948.

Palestine?
A region within the Middle East with religious importance to Muslims, Christians and Jews. It now falls within an area covered by Israel and the Palestinian Authority territories of the West Bank and the Gaza Strip.

No lasting peace can be found until the quarrel between Israel and the Palestinian people is resolved

15

Israel and Occupied Territories

Has Palestine ever been an independent state?

No. It has generally fallen under the control of other empires or polities. During the 20th century the region has, in whole or in part, been governed by the Ottoman Empire, the UK, Israel, Jordan, Egypt and the Palestinian Authority.

Why have Arab countries historically opposed Israel?

For partly political, partly religious reasons. Israel is viewed as a state thrust upon the region by Western interests. It is also a Jewish state in a region whose population is mainly Muslim.

Major wars occurred between the two sides in 1948, 1956, 1967 and 1973 – clashes that still resonate and shape the region today. And although relations have eased since the late 1970s, no lasting peace can be found until the quarrel between Israel and the Palestinian people is resolved.

Why are Israel and the Palestinians in dispute?

Following the wars of 1948 and 1967, Israel annexed and occupied land that the Palestinians believe is rightfully theirs. Palestinians have been driven from their homes and forced to live abroad or with restricted freedom in areas such as the Gaza Strip and the West Bank. At the same time Israel has encouraged Jewish immigrants to settle within these areas.

So it is a conflict about land?
In the main, though religion plays a role. The majority of Israelis (77%) are Jewish. The majority of Palestinians (97%) are Muslim. The religious argument is centred over who has control of Jerusalem, a city of spiritual importance to both faiths.

Have Israel and the Palestinians ever come close to peace?
The Oslo Accords of 1993, overseen by President Clinton, were a high-water mark in relations between the two sides but during the 1990s these Accords crumbled. The current peace initiative, the 2002 Roadmap for Peace, appears increasingly ineffectual.

The Arab League, driven by Saudi Arabia, have also issued a peace proposal to Israel, first in Beirut in 2002 and latterly re-issued in Riyadh in 2007. Israel's response has been lukewarm.

MIDDLE EAST CONFLICT – THE ISSUES

The Arab-Israeli conflict began with Israel's creation in 1948. However, fighting between Jewish immigrants and the native Arabs stretches back to the late 19th century.

There have been four major wars between the two sides – 1948, 1956, 1967 and 1973.

At the heart of the conflict is a dispute between Israel and the Palestinian people.

Land is the key issue in this conflict, though religion does play its part.

Israel and the Palestinians came closest to peace with the Oslo Accords of 1993.

THE MIDDLE EAST AND THE WEST

The Cold War pulled Western nations into the Arab-Israeli conflict. Since its end, the Middle East's abundant oil and gas supplies and the rise of Islamist militant movements in the region have continued to draw Western attention.

THE COLD WAR

What was the Cold War?
It was a period of conflict, tension and rivalry between the USA and the Soviet Union from the end of the Second World War in 1945 until the collapse of the Soviet Union in the early 1990s.

Western nations looked to prevent the spread of communism in the Middle East by nurturing strategic allies in the region. Israel has been the West's most long-standing and consistent ally.

Was Israel the West's only ally in the Middle East?
No, support was provided to Saudi Arabia from the 1960s onwards whilst Egypt also became a key ally from the late 1970s. Turkey has consistently been an ally, whilst even Iran was supported by the USA until the Shah was toppled by the Islamic Revolution of 1979.

Why did the West, and most importantly the USA, support Israel?
A shared commitment to democracy was one cornerstone. Another was the strong Jewish – often termed "Zionist" – political pressure exerted in many Western countries. Finally, sympathy and possibly guilt at the extent of the Nazi Holocaust during the Second World War affected political decisions.

What happened at the end of the Cold War?
The collapse of the Soviet Union crossed with the rise of a new global movement, Islamist militancy. Faced with this, Western nations have continued to support their allies in the region, hoping they can act as a bulwark against militancy.

ISLAMIST MILITANCY

What is Islamist militancy?
Groups such as Al Qaeda, Hamas or Hezbollah have been involved in frequent attacks against Israeli or Western targets across the world – Al Qaeda cells were responsible for the 9/11 attacks on the USA in 2001, the London bombings of 7/7 in 2005 and Islamist militants were again behind the foiled attacks in London and Glasgow in 2007. Both Hamas and Hezbollah have been responsible for suicide bomb attacks within Israeli cities. Certain countries, for example Iran, are suspected by the West of funding and equipping some of these militant groups.

Isn't this just terrorism?
It is in the eyes of many, including Western governments. However, to most Palestinians on the ground in Gaza and the West Bank, and to many Arabs, some attacks are viewed as legitimate acts of resistance against hostile Western powers and supporters of Israel.

What drives Islamist militants?
There is no straightforward answer. The plight of the Palestinians is one cause but not the only one. Others include the destruction of Israel, the removal of Western influence in the Middle East, and the desire to spread Sharia law globally.

Would solving the Israeli-Palestinian conflict stop militant attacks?
Probably not, since the aims of the militants are so varied and complex. However, a peaceful solution to the conflict between Israel and the Arab world, and particularly the Palestinians, may go some way towards preventing moderate Muslim opinion from drifting towards the extremes.

Has moderate Muslim opinion been affected in the UK?
A recent poll of Muslims in the UK showed that a fifth had sympathy with the "feelings and motives" of those behind the London bombings of 7th July 2005. Although reasons for this response are not down to a single issue, the Israeli-Palestinian dispute has been a constant, high-profile grievance.

Did militant attacks occur before the rise of the Islamists?

Yes. The secular Palestinian Liberation Organisation (PLO) brought their cause to the attention of the world through terrorist attacks. One famous example was the hijacking of the Achille Lauro sea liner in 1985 and a number of commercial flights during the 1970s and 1980s. A group linked to the PLO was behind the murder of Israeli athletes at the 1972 Munich Olympics.

On the other side, Jewish groups have also been involved in terrorism. In 1946, a Jewish militant group bombed Jerusalem's King David Hotel, the seat of British government in the region at the time, to press their case for an independent Jewish state.

THE ROLE OF OIL

How much oil and gas is there in the Middle East?

It is estimated that the region has two-thirds of the world's remaining oil and over 40% of its gas, though none of this resides in Israel or the Palestinian territories.

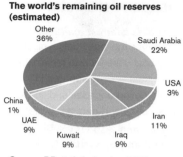

The world's remaining oil reserves (estimated)

Source: BP statistical review 2006

Why is Middle Eastern oil and gas important to the West?

Many Western countries have their own oil or gas reserves but they are finite and being depleted quickly, under pressure from ever increasing energy demands. For example, the UK was, until recently, self-sufficient in natural gas. We now need to import gas to meet our needs and by 2020 it is thought that the UK will have to import 90% of its gas.

As a result Western countries are looking at new ways to power themselves both in response to global warming and a wish to be energy "secure" – witness the UK's plans to invest in a second generation of nuclear power stations and new renewable energy sources, such as wind farms.

However, the fossil fuels – oil, gas and coal – are likely to remain the dominant energy sources in forthcoming decades and, in the case of oil and gas, the Middle East will be an increasingly important player in this market.

What's wrong with relying on the Middle East for oil and gas?
It's an issue of supply. If interrupted, or the world markets worry about the security of supply, then prices tend to rise. When the price of oil goes up it affects the cost of living, forcing up inflation and compromising economic growth.

How could an Arab-Israeli conflict affect oil prices?
If the conflict spilled into neighbouring countries then world markets would naturally become twitchy. Another fear is that if the West becomes too reliant on Middle East oil and gas it could expose it to the danger of "political" interference in its supply.

One telling example was the Arab-Israeli war of 1973. Arab countries put an embargo on oil exports to those countries supporting Israel, including the USA and UK. The ensuing crisis was the catalyst for a global recession the following year.

THE MIDDLE EAST AND THE WEST – THE ISSUES

The West has been involved in the Middle East for decades.

Israel was considered a strategic buffer against Soviet influence and more recently against the spread of Islamist militancy.

The existence of Israel in the region and the plight of the Palestinians are important, though not the sole, motivations for Islamist militants.

The Middle East is important because it has the largest remaining oil reserves in the world.

ISRAEL AND THE PALESTINIANS – THE OBSTACLES TO PEACE

Over the past thirty years the Arab-Israeli conflict has become increasingly concentrated on the dispute between Israel and the Palestinians. *Pocket Issue* looks at the core issues dividing the two sides and asks whether the leaders can ever be "partners in peace".

THE CURRENT SITUATION

What is the current situation?
In 2005, Israel pulled out of the Gaza Strip that it had occupied during the 1967 war. It continues to expand its presence in the West Bank. Both the Gaza Strip and the West Bank are nominally under the control of the Palestinian Authority which has been fractured by in-fighting between the two leading Palestinian political parties, Hamas and Fatah. Hamas now effectively controls the Gaza Strip, Fatah the West Bank.

Israel controls the borders into the Occupied Territories and there is little freedom of movement for Palestinians within the West Bank.

The Gaza strip

The West Bank

JEWISH SETTLEMENTS

What is the issue with Jewish settlements?
Following the wars of 1967 and 1973 (see *A brief history*), Jewish immigrants began to build homes in the newly occupied and annexed territories forcing Palestinians from their land. They were supported by an Israeli military presence.

What is the world's view on the Jewish settlements in these areas?
The UN Security Council stated that they had "no legal validity." Despite this Israel continued to expand the settlements, especially in the West Bank.

The oft-quoted UN resolutions are 242 (issued after the 1967 war) and 338 (issued after the 1973 war). Both called for Israel to withdraw from the territories it occupied in 1967.

How many Jews settled in these areas?
Up to 9,000 in the Gaza Strip, over 400,000 in the West Bank and East Jerusalem.

23

Why did the settlers want to move into hostile areas?
Some moved after financial encouragement from the Israeli government, who, some argue, want to extend and consolidate Israeli control of these areas. However many Jewish settlers have been driven by religious conviction since several Jewish holy areas fall within the West Bank (the lands of Judea and Samaria).

Why did Israel not annex Gaza and the West Bank within its own borders?
It would undermine the "Jewishness" of Israel. There are 3.7 million Palestinians in these areas, mostly Muslim.

Hasn't Israel begun to remove Jewish settlers from these territories?
Partly. In 2005, under the leadership of Ariel Sharon, Jewish settlers were removed – many kicking and screaming – from the Gaza Strip and from tiny settlements in the northern West Bank.

Why did Israel do this?
Many view it as a political move. Jewish settlements in the Gaza Strip were small-fry compared to those in the West Bank and Israel has more political interest invested in the latter. It also provided a high-profile response to the 2002 Roadmap to Peace which advocated, once again, Israeli withdrawal from Gaza and the West Bank.

So has this eased relations?
Not really. Between 2004 and 2005 the overall number of settlers increased, despite the planned Gaza withdrawals. Israel also continues to control Gaza's borders, sea and air space.

Palestinians are also aggrieved that Israel pulled out of Gaza without any discussion with the Palestinian Authority, viewing this as further evidence of Israeli arrogance and its inability to work in partnership.

Between 2004 and 2005 the overall number of settlers increased in the Occupied Territories, despite the Gaza withdrawals.

Does Israel intend to withdraw from its settlements in the West Bank?

It's highly unlikely. Israel would want to swallow chunks of the West Bank in any final settlement of borders. Moreover, some settlements are the size of small cities and not easily dismantled. For example, the settlement of Ma'ale Adumim in the West Bank has a population of over 34,000.

THE PALESTINIAN "RIGHT OF RETURN"

What is the background to the Palestinian "right of return"?

The Palestinians lost land to Israel in the 1948 war and also in the wake of the 1967 war, which heralded the start of the Jewish settlements in the Occupied Territories. In principle, the Palestinians wish to return to these lands.

Do the Palestinians really want to return?

Probably not. Many Palestinians are now settled in other countries, both in the Middle East and beyond, though there are still

> Palestinians want "just" compensation for land lost to Jewish immigrants over the past sixty years

many poorer Palestinians in refugee camps in countries such as Lebanon, Jordan and elsewhere.

Although the lost land is an emotional issue for Palestinians, they are more likely to want some type of "just" compensation for lands lost to Jewish immigrants over the past sixty years.

How many Palestinians are classed as refugees?

The official number is just over four million. This includes people displaced in 1948 and 1967 and their descendants. Most live in the West Bank, the Gaza Strip and Jordan. Syria and Lebanon also have large Palestinian populations.

Why would a return to 1948 lands be unlikely?

It is unacceptable to Israel.

25

An influx of Palestinians would put pressure on available land for Jews as well as diluting the Jewish character of Israel. There is also the practical legal issue of sorting through thousands of rival claims over land.

Has Israel ever tried to re-integrate Palestinians?
Israel offered a limited return to 75,000 refugee Palestinians in 1949 (in the aftermath of the 1948 war). This was only around 10% of the total refugees created by that war. Currently, nearly 20% of Israel's population is Arab.

And do Arabs and Jews have equal rights in Israel?
In principle, yes (though not in the Occupied Territories). Arabs have freedom of religion, culture and political organisation (there are Arab political parties in the

Knesset, the Israeli Parliament).

Some observers feel that this picture is less rosy in practice. In 2004 the US state department noted that Israel did "little to reduce institutional, legal and societal discrimination against the Arab citizens". A recent UN report saw shadows of apartheid in the relationship between Jews and Arabs within Israel.

Hasn't Israel already offered compensation to the Palestinians displaced in 1948?
In 1950 it passed the Israeli Absentee Property Law that allowed compensation to be paid to Palestinians for lost land. Very few Palestinians took this up, viewing it as a means to legitimise an illegal occupation.

Has the "right of return" proved a stumbling block to peace?
One reason that the Oslo Accords of 1993 made progress was that the "right of return" was put to one side and not discussed. When placed back on the table at Camp David in 2000, it contributed to talks collapsing.

A recent UN report saw shadows of apartheid in the relationship between Jews and Arabs in Israel

The Arab League's peace initiative, first issued in 2002 and revived in 2007, also calls for a "just solution" for Palestinian refugees before "normal relations" can be established with Israel.

JERUSALEM

Why is Jerusalem such a key city for both Israelis and Palestinians?

Religious importance. For Jews, it is their "eternal and undivided" capital. The bond goes back to King Solomon and the building of the First Temple of Jerusalem on Temple Mount in the 10th century BC. Zionism stems from one of Jerusalem's names (Zion).

For Muslims, Jerusalem contains the Al-Aqsa Mosque, the third holiest site in Islam. Jerusalem was also, briefly, the first direction of prayer before Mecca.

The Temple Mount and the Muslim Noble Sanctuary (which contains the Al-Aqsa Mosque) basically cover the same area of land. This falls within the area of East Jerusalem.

Jerusalem

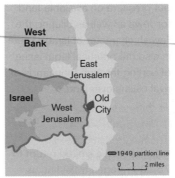

Who currently controls Jerusalem?

Israel. Until 1948, Jerusalem was under control of the British Mandate. After the 1948 war, Israel controlled West Jerusalem, and Jordan East Jerusalem. After the 1967 war, East Jerusalem was annexed by Israel and new Jewish settlements soon grew in the area.

What was the UN's initial intention for Jerusalem in 1947?

That it fell under UN governance. The 1948 war put paid to that.

What do both sides want?

Israel says Jerusalem is its capital city. That this is not recognised by the UN is illustrated by the fact that national embassies are

27

based in Tel Aviv rather than Jerusalem. The Palestinians want East Jerusalem as the capital of a Palestinian state.

BORDERS

Is there an agreed outline for a Palestinian state?
The most often quoted is that Israel should withdraw to the borders it held before the 1967 War. However, this picture is complicated by both Israeli and Palestinian ambitions and the existing, large Jewish settlements in the West Bank.

Does Israel currently have defined borders?
No. Decades of fighting with its Arab neighbours has led to a number of contentious areas, such as in the West Bank or the

Golan Heights between Israel and Syria. On coming to power in 2006, Israeli Prime Minister, Ehud Olmert, stated that his priority was to decide Israel's final borders.

What will guide Israel's decision on borders?
Two factors. Firstly, security and the prevention of Palestinian or foreign attacks on the country. Secondly, maintaining the Jewish nature of the country. Israeli government policy aims to include the large settlements in the West Bank within its borders.

What do the Palestinians want?
Palestinians believe that for Palestine to be an effective country there needs to be a geographic link between the Gaza Strip and the West Bank – this is one of their key demands. Since this would need to cut across Israeli territory this is unlikely to be rubber-stamped by Israel.

Furthermore, within the West Bank, Palestinians do not want the land broken up by Jewish settlements. They want territorial

> Israeli Prime Minister, Ehud Olmert, stated that his priority was to decide Israel's final borders

28

contiguity not disconnected chunks of land. For example, the settlement of Ma'ale Adumim has grown so much that it now virtually cuts the West Bank in two.

The Israeli Security Barrier

Why has Israel been building a "barrier" in the West Bank?
Israel calls it a "fence" and declares that it is for maintaining security and preventing attacks against Israel. However, Palestinians describe it a "wall" and view it as a land-grab, since the barrier encompasses nearly 10% of the total area of the West Bank.

It also has an impact on the everyday lives of Palestinians who are divided by it from their jobs and, in some cases, have seen their communities split asunder.

Some commentators have questioned whether the "barrier" is part of an overall Israeli policy to "Balkanise" the Palestinian territories and to prevent a stable Palestinian state being established.

STRENGTH OF LEADERSHIP

What is the issue with leadership?
A common phrase in Israel-Palestinian peace talks is the need for both sides to be "partners in peace". Israel doubts that the Palestinian leadership has the ability or will to fill this role, especially when Hamas is involved. In turn, the Palestinian Authority questions Israel's determination to settle the dispute equitably.

The outcome of this mistrust tends to be "tit-for-tat" aggression that often spirals into one of the other clichés commonly ascribed to the region, the "cycle of violence".

But what are the challenges facing the leadership of both sides?

THE PALESTINIAN AUTHORITY

Does the Palestinian leadership want peace with Israel?
The two main parties are Fatah and Hamas. Fatah has accepted the "two-state" solution since 1988. Hamas has moved from wanting the immediate destruction of Israel to creating a state based on pre-1967 borders in return for offering Israel a long-term truce. They still do not formally recognise Israel's right to exist in the region.

What is Fatah?
Fatah (Reverse Arabic acronym: Movement for the Liberation of Palestine) has traditionally been the party of power, dominating both the PLO and the early days of the Palestinian Authority. It was the party of Yasser Arafat. Fatah has both a political and paramilitary wing, though, unlike Hamas, it is not viewed as a terrorist organisation by the West and is a secular movement. Though not an Islamist militant group, it has links to groups who have carried out suicide bomb attacks in the past decade.

What is Hamas?
Hamas (Arabic: *zeal*) is a Sunni Islamist militant group. It gained popularity in the late 1980s and 1990s due to its uncompromising attitude to Israel (which it doesn't recognise) and its welfare support for the Palestinians. It has both a political and paramilitary wing, the latter responsible for many suicide bomb attacks in Israel. It is viewed as a terrorist organisation by many Western nations.

What control does the Palestinian Authority officially have?
Set up as an interim government following the Oslo Accords in 1993, its powers vary, from both military and civil control in some Palestinian areas to no control whatsoever in East Jerusalem.

Hamas holds the power in Gaza and Fatah grips the reins in the West Bank

Is the Palestinian Authority the same as the PLO?

No. The PLO is an older institution – initially established in 1964 – that brought together several Palestinian factions under one umbrella. Due to its central place in the history of the conflict, the PLO is still the official voice of the Palestinian people, for example within the UN.

What are Hamas and Fatah fighting about?

Control. Hamas won a Palestinian parliamentary election in 2006 mainly due to Palestinian dismay at both the corruption and inefficiency of Fatah-led government. Although a national unity government was proclaimed in March 2007, it was dissolved in the wake of the heavy fighting three months later in June 2007.

Can the Palestinians provide Israel with a "partner for peace"?

The focus should be on the Palestinian Authority. However, since the factional fighting of 2007 the government has been split, with Hamas holding power in Gaza and Fatah gripping the reins in the West Bank.

The USA and the Israelis are now focussing on the Fatah-run Palestinian Authority in the West Bank, hoping to isolate Hamas.

Are the Fatah and Hamas leaderships able to control the Occupied Territories?

It is doubted by many observers. Even the parties themselves are further split by factions and in-fighting. Guns seem to be readily available and much of the trouble is down to turf-wars and local score settling. This is not helped by the very poor socio-economic conditions that exist in the Occupied Territories.

What is life like for Palestinians in the Occupied Territories?

Hard. Many Palestinians are poor and lacking in opportunities.

The World Bank compared the recession caused by the Second Intifada (2000-05) as comparable to the 1929 Wall Street Crash for the Palestinian economy. Over half of Palestinians are unemployed and two-thirds live below the poverty line.

Why is the Palestinian economy so weak?

It is very reliant on Israel, especially to provide jobs to the Palestinian people. When Israel clamps down due to security concerns – creating checkpoints or erecting "security fences" – it undermines the basic working of the economy.

Furthermore, Israel controls the Palestinian air, land and (in Gaza's case) sea links to the outside world so it cannot trade effectively. Some commentators have likened the Occupied Territories to open prisons.

However, blame does not lie solely with Israel. The Palestinian Authority is also accused of being corrupt and inefficient.

How is the Palestinian Authority funded?

It relies on tax and custom revenues collected by Israel and aid from the international community. When Hamas was elected in 2006, aid was withheld as Hamas was viewed as a "terrorist" organisation. The aim of this policy was to either bring Hamas to the table or bring it down; in fact it seems to have only worsened the lot of the Palestinians.

How big an issue is Palestinian poverty?

One UN report noted: "A viable Palestinian economy is a pre-requisite for any meaningful two-state solution to the Middle East conflict" but adds that currently "the economy is barely functioning".

ISRAEL

What is the political situation in Israel?

Israel is divided in its approach. At a very simplified level the right-wing, represented by parties such as Likud, sees meeting force with force as the best way forward. The left-wing, led by the Israeli Labour party, is often more open to dialogue. In practice the divide is less clear-cut.

In 2005, Ariel Sharon created the new centre-right party Kadima, asserting that Israel would need to give up land to maintain its position. However, East Jerusalem and the larger West Bank settlements would stay under Israeli control. Ehud Olmert, the current Prime Minister, who replaced Sharon as Kadima's leader in 2006, saw that "painful concessions" were needed.

What does Israel want?
Peace, but on its own terms. It has legitimate concerns about its security – with regular suicide and rocket attacks over the past decade – and maintains an active policy of trying to assassinate leaders of militant groups. Some commentators also feel that Israel would not favour a buoyant Palestinian economy on its doorstep, leading it to continue to enforce harmful security checks and the building of the West Bank "barrier".

OBSTACLES TO PEACE – THE ISSUES

The Israeli-Palestinian peace process continues to flounder.

Jewish settlements in the West Bank are perhaps the most controversial area.

The Palestinians want compensation for land lost following the 1948 and 1967 wars.

Both sides want control of East Jerusalem.

The borders for a "two-state" solution are still unclear and disputed.

The Palestinian economy is on its knees. Improving conditions in Gaza and the West Bank may be an essential part of any peace process.

Fighting between Hamas and Fatah has led to the Palestinian territories and its leadership being split.

THE ARAB-ISRAELI CONFLICT – A BRIEF HISTORY

Much of the conflict between Israel and the Arab world is rooted in a past that has encompassed aggression, bad faith, foreign meddling and some vision. *Pocket Issue* offers a crash course in the history behind the conflict.

UP TO 1948 – ISRAEL IS FOUNDED

Key dates at a glance

135AD Jews expelled from Judea by the Romans. The beginnings of the Jewish diaspora.

1882 First wave of Jewish immigration to the Ottoman province of Palestine.

1916 Arab Revolt against the Ottomans.

1917 Balfour Declaration.

1920 Beginning of the British Mandate over Palestine.

1936-39 Arab Revolt against the British.

1939-45 The Jewish Holocaust.

1947 UN Partition Plan for Palestine.

14th May 1948 Israel proclaims itself a state.

15th May 1948 End of the British Mandate in Palestine.

What is the key date in the history of the conflict?
Arguably, 14th May 1948, the day Israel was founded.

Were there Jews living in the region of Palestine prior to that date?
By 1948, about a third of the population of Palestine was Jewish. From 1882 onwards there were a number of waves of Jewish immigration into Palestine, what the Jewish people call Aliyahs (Hebrew: *ascent*). The Jews were mainly arriving from eastern Europe and Russia as growing anti-semitism forced them to flee.

Anti-semitism?
Prejudice and hostility towards the Jewish people. This anti-semitism reached its height following the policies of Hitler's Germany during the 1930s.

Why did the Jewish people wish to live in Palestine?
Because historically the area was the first, and only, Kingdom of Israel. A yearning to return had been a major theme in Jewish religious and political thought for centuries. This gained momentum with the Zionist movement that began in the late 19th century.

What is a Zionist?
Zionism refers to the Biblical connection between the Jewish people and the land of Israel (Zion is one name for Jerusalem). In the late 19th century, a modern Zionist movement, founded by the Hungarian Theodor Herzl, became a powerful focus and lobbying group for Jewish ambitions. Its main aim was the establishment of a Jewish state within the borders of Palestine. Relentless Zionist pressure proved one of the most important factors in the creation of Israel.

What had originally forced the Jews to leave the region?
It goes back to 135AD, when the Romans destroyed Jerusalem in the process of crushing a Jewish revolt. This is

By 1948, about a third of the population of Palestine was Jewish

often viewed as the start of the Jewish diaspora, as Jews were forced to flee abroad or were sold into slavery.

Who governed Palestine at the end of the 19th century?
Palestine was a province in the Ottoman (Turkish) Empire. The loose rule of the Ottomans in the region initially encouraged Jewish immigration from Europe. Ottoman governance continued until the First World War (1914-18) when the British entered the picture.

How did the British become involved in Palestine?
The Ottoman Empire aligned itself with the Germans during the First World War. The British encouraged the Arabs in Palestine to revolt against the Ottomans, leading to the Arab Revolt of 1916. In return the

Arabs were led to believe that the British would support an independent Arab state at the end of the war. However in 1917, the British government struck against this "promise" with the Balfour Declaration.

The Balfour Declaration?
Historians argue over what exactly Balfour (then British Foreign Secretary) intended for Palestine. But essentially, the Declaration recognised the rights of Jews to a homeland in Palestine, with the proviso that the rights of the existing Arab population were also recognised. It became embedded in policy once Palestine came under the British Mandate in 1920.

What was the British Mandate?
At the end of the war in 1918, and following the collapse of the Ottoman Empire, Palestine was put under the care of Britain by the League of Nations (the forerunner to the United Nations) for a fixed period. The Mandate and the Balfour Declaration encouraged new waves of Jewish immigration to the area. Iraq and Jordan were

> It is estimated that between five and seven million Jews were killed during the Nazi Holocaust

also under British Mandate. Syria and Lebanon fell under a French mandate.

How did the Arab population of Palestine respond?
Angrily. Riots took place throughout the 1920s. Increased Jewish immigration from Nazi Germany in the 1930s raised tensions, with atrocities committed by both sides. It eventually led to a second Arab Revolt between 1936-39. This uprising was eventually crushed by British forces, supported by armed Jewish police and a Jewish military organisation, the Haganah (Hebrew: *defence*) which later formed the core of the Israeli army.

One tragic postscript to this period was that, in response to the Revolt, the British limited

Jewish immigration into Palestine at exactly the time that the Nazi Holocaust began to gain momentum.

What was the extent of the Nazi Holocaust?

During the Second World War (1939-45), it is estimated that between five and seven million Jews were killed in concentration camps, labour camps, ghettos, and on the Russian front through the German policy of exterminating Jews. It is believed that 60% of European Jews and 35% of Jews worldwide were murdered.

Did the Holocaust force the creation of Israel?

Not primarily. There had always been the intention for some kind of Jewish state once the British mandate expired in 1948. The Zionist lobby had played a crucial role in pushing for this and their hand was strengthened by international reaction to the Holocaust.

A 1947 plan – developed by the newly created UN – saw Palestine divided into two states.

The Jewish area consisted of 55% of the land, the Arab area roughly 45%, despite the fact that Arabs outnumbered Jews two-to-one. Jerusalem was to fall under UN jurisdiction.

1947 UN partition plan

37

How did Jews and Arabs respond to the Partition Plan?

The majority of Jews – despite opposition from extreme Jewish nationalist groups – accepted the proposal. The Arabs, unhappy at what they viewed as an unfair division of the land, rejected the plan and the legitimacy of Israel. Fighting broke out almost immediately.

Was the 1947 UN partition plan ever implemented?

No. Britain viewed it as unworkable and had already decided to withdraw troops from Palestine. With a power vacuum looming and international procrastination, Jewish leaders unilaterally declared the State of Israel on 14th May 1948 (the day before Britain was due to terminate its mandate).

> During the conflict of 1948/9, over 700,000 Palestinians fled Palestine

1948 TO 1973 – ISRAEL EXPANDS HER BORDERS

Key dates at a glance

1948/9 First Arab-Israeli War and the Nakba.

1956 The Suez Crisis.

1964 Foundation of the PLO.

1967 The "Six Day" War.

1970 Black September in Jordan.

1973 The "Yom Kippur" War.

1979 Israel-Egypt peace treaty.

What was the reaction of the Arab world to the creation of Israel?

Hostility. In 1948 a coalition of Arab states attacked Israel. This included Iraq, Egypt, Syria, Lebanon, and Transjordan (what is now Jordan).

Who won this war?

Israel, with financial support from the USA and military aid from a then-friendly Czechoslovakia. By the time an armistice was signed in 1949, Israel had taken nearly 80% of the land intended for the Palestinians in the now defunct UN plan of 1947.

What happened to the Palestinians?

During the conflict of 1948-49, over 700,000 Palestinians fled Palestine (two-thirds of the total Arab Palestinian population), fearing Israeli violence. Palestinians called this exodus the Nakba (Arabic: *catastrophe*).

Was any land left for the Palestinian Arabs?

Not much. It was occupied by Jordan (East Jerusalem and the West Bank) and Egypt (the Gaza Strip) after the 1949 truce agreements. Neither Jordan nor Egypt was prepared to allow the Palestinians to form a state on land under their control.

So what happened to the lands that Israel occupied during the 1948/9 war?

Generally they were passed to Jewish immigrants, whose numbers rapidly increased after the war. One of the founding principles of the Israeli state is the "right of return", allowing Jewish people of whatever background to come and live in Israel.

How many new immigrants came to Israel?

Nearly 700,000, doubling Israel's population within one year of its establishment. Survivors of the Holocaust, refugees from an anti-semitic Soviet Union, Jews from North Africa and the Middle East fleeing hostile Arab nations, and the promise of prosperity and acceptance swelled their numbers.

Were the Palestinian refugees allowed to return to their lands?

In 1949 the Israelis offered to allow 75,000 Palestinians back, a tenth of those who had fled. The Arab nations rejected the proposal but nevertheless it is thought that between 30,000 and 90,000 refugees attempted to return "illegally", despite Israeli attempts to stop them.

Why did Israel block the return of Palestinians?

They did not want the Jewish nature of their new state to be swamped by the returning Palestinians, most of whom were Muslim. There were also practical considerations, most notably the need to house the huge numbers of Jews moving into the country.

Suez marked the wane of British influence in the Middle East

Did Israel offer the Palestinians anything in return?

A law in 1950 was passed offering compensation to be paid to Palestinians for their land. The Palestinians saw this as a ploy to legalise what they viewed as an illegal occupation and only a few hundred Palestinians accepted payment.

Was that the end of the fighting?

No. Fighting was almost continuous between Israel and its neighbours. Two events brought wider international involvement; the Suez Crisis of 1956 and the Arab-Israeli War of 1967.

What was the Suez Crisis?

It was nominally centred on control of the Suez Canal but was played out against the backdrop of Cold War politics and also the end of colonial rule in the Middle East. Colonel Nasser of Egypt had taken control of the Suez Canal. The UK, the most recent imperial power in Egypt, together with France and Israel, hatched a plan to attack Nasser. They attacked, but lacking American and wider international backing, were soon forced to withdraw.

What were the long-term effects of the Suez Crisis?

Israel's initial military successes gained it the reputation as the region's "superpower". Britain and France's importance in the region waned and was replaced by the USA, which was looking to counter Soviet influence in the area. Nasser's brand of assertive Arab nationalism grew in popularity, eventually leading to the establishment of the PLO.

What happened in the 1967 Arab-Israeli War?

The 1967 war – often called the "Six Day War" – was a battle between Israel and, principally, Egypt, Jordan and Syria. Faced with the threat of economic suffocation by the Arab nations, Israel took dramatic pre-emptive action and won a crushing victory.

What were the main outcomes of the 1967 war?

It shaped the geography of the dispute up to the present day. Israel took the Gaza Strip from Egypt and the West Bank from Jordan. These areas become known as the Occupied Territories. Israel also annexed East Jerusalem, took the Golan Heights from Syria and temporarily occupied the Sinai Peninsula from Egypt. Jewish settlement began in these areas almost immediately.

The war also led to a more militant line being taken by the PLO under Yasser Arafat, who took control of the organisation in 1969. This was primarily aimed at Israel but also caused turbulence in other Arab states, for example during Black September in Jordan in 1970.

Black September?

A bloody "civil" war between Jordanian forces and the Palestinian groups who had moved to Jordan. It eventually led to the PLO being forced to move its headquarters and leadership to Lebanon.

What led to the Yom Kippur War of 1973?

In October 1973, Egypt and Syria attacked Israel on the Jewish holiday of Yom Kippur aiming to regain lands lost in 1967. This time there was no crushing victory for either side.

What were the long-term effects of the 1973 War?

It broke Israel's aura of invincibility and led to the Camp David Accords of 1978 and a full peace treaty the following year, when Egypt became the first Arab nation to recognise Israel. The Sinai Peninsula eventually returned under full Egyptian control in 1982 with the few Jewish settlements being dismantled.

> The 1967 War shaped the geography of the dispute to the present day

1980 TO 2000 – THE ROAD TO OSLO AND BEYOND

Key dates at a glance

1982 Israel invades Lebanon.

1987-93 First Intifada.

1988 Palestinian "Algiers" declaration recognises "two-state" solution.

1991 First Gulf War following Iraq's invasion of Kuwait.

1991 Madrid Conference.

1993 Oslo Accords between Israel and the PLO.

Have Israel and the Palestinians ever been close to peace?
The high point in relations came with the Oslo Accords of 1993. The PLO recognised Israel's right to live in peace and security, and both sides committed to a process of negotiation intended to lead to a permanent settlement. It also established the Palestinian Authority to govern these territories.

How did that affect the wider Arab world?
In the wake of Oslo, many Arab nations became less hostile towards Israel. Some, like Jordan, established diplomatic relations. Others, such as Syria, saw face-to-face talks come to nothing.

How did Oslo come about?
Following the Gulf War in 1991 – triggered by Saddam Hussein's invasion of Kuwait – the international community tried to bring Israel and its Arab neighbours closer together through the Madrid Conference of 1991. Deadlock at Madrid saw the start of secret, unofficial negotiations between Israel and the PLO in Oslo.

How had relations between Israel and the PLO developed since the 1970s?
Initially badly. Ongoing fighting led Israel to invade Lebanon in 1982, where the PLO now based its leadership. As with Jordan in 1970, the PLO had formed a "state-within-a-state" in Lebanon. The PLO was forced to withdraw to Tunisia. Israel remained in occupation until 2000.

What about Israel's relations with other Arab nations?
Not calm. For example in 1981 the Israeli air force bombed a nuclear plant in Iraq believing Saddam Hussein was developing nuclear weapons with which to attack Israel.

Was Oslo the first time that the Palestinians recognised Israel?
No. The Palestinian National Council (a government-in-exile dominated by the PLO) voted to support a "two-state" solution at a conference in Algiers in 1988, with Israel withdrawing back to its pre-1967 borders. It was the first time that the Palestinians had recognised the right of Israel to exist in the region.

Did this proclamation mark the end of violence?
No. The First Intifada (Arabic: *uprising*) took place in the Gaza Strip and the West Bank between 1987 and 1993. It stemmed from frustration within the Palestinian community at the slow progress of both its humanitarian and nationalist aims. Taking the exiled PLO leadership by surprise, it also

saw the emergence of Hamas. Nearly 200 Israelis and 2,000 Palestinians were killed during this period (some by their own side accused of "collaborating").

2000 TO THE PRESENT DAY – OSLO UNRAVELS

Key dates at a glance

2000 Camp David Summit.

2001 Taba Summit.

2000-05 Second (Al-Aqsa) Intifada.

2002 Roadmap for Peace issued.

2005 Israel withdraws from the Gaza Strip.

2006 Israel enters Lebanon.

2007 Factional fighting in the Occupied Territories.

How did the Oslo Accords fare?
Despite initial optimism, Oslo stalled at the negotiating table. It was not helped by the assassination of Yitzhak Rabin, the Israeli Prime Minister and signature at Oslo, in 1995.

It finally broke down at the Camp David Summit of 2000, when Clinton, Arafat and then Israeli PM Ehud Barak failed to come to agreement. One final attempt in the last days of the Clinton administration, at Taba in 2001, came close but failed to break the deadlock.

Why did Oslo falter?
Those four central issues: Jewish settlements, the "right of return", East Jerusalem and borders. They were not discussed at Oslo but left to future negotiation. Once tabled again, they led to the agreement collapsing.

Was there further fighting?
Yes, the Second (Al-Aqsa) Intifada from 2000-05, Al-Aqsa being the Noble Sanctuary mosque in Jerusalem. A controversial visit in 2000 by Ariel Sharon (soon to become Israel's PM) to the Temple Mount triggered the conflict though it also reflected a wider frustration at the stalling peace process. Over 4,000 Palestinians and 1,000 Israelis were killed.

Have there been any further peace initiatives since the start of the Al-Aqsa Intifada in 2000?
The main one is the Roadmap for Peace, established in June 2002. It called for a Palestinian state side-by-side with Israel, the end of Palestinian aggression and Israel's withdrawal and freezing of settlement activities in the Occupied Territories.

Who proposed the 2002 Roadmap?
The UN, USA, European Union and Russia – referred to as the "Quartet".

How is the Roadmap prospering?
Pretty poorly. Israel withdrew its presence from the Gaza Strip in 2005, but continued settlement activity in the West Bank. It is also constructing its "barrier" along a controversial path through West Bank territory and has made regular incursions into the Palestinian territories. Palestinian militants have continued to attack Israel, despite a 16-month ceasefire following the Roadmap's first publication.

Any other peace initiatives?
The other main one is the Saudi-led Arab League initiative, sometimes referred to as King Abdullah's peace plan. It was first proposed in Beirut in 2002, and re-issued in Riyadh in 2007.

It called for the withdrawal of Israel from Gaza and the West Bank, a Palestinian state with East Jerusalem as its capital and a "just solution" for Palestinian refugees. In return it would consider the conflict with Israel over and would establish "normal relations".

Israel has given it a lukewarm reception without completely turning its back.

Are there any new problems?
Two main ones: Vicious factional fighting within the Palestinian territories during 2007 between Fatah and Hamas, and Israel entering Lebanon in 2006.

What happened in Lebanon?
Israeli troops fought a short and unsuccessful campaign against Hezbollah in southern Lebanon.

What is Hezbollah?
A Shia Islamist militant group with a power base in southern Lebanon. They first came to the fore fighting Israel's occupation of southern Lebanon after the 1982 invasion. They have continued to launch rocket attacks upon Israel.

A BRIEF HISTORY – THE ISSUES

The key dates in the shaping of Israel were the 1948 and 1967 Arab-Israeli wars.

The Israel-Palestinian crisis sits at the heart of the wider conflict.

Israel wants its existence respected. The Palestinians want a homeland.

The closest the sides have come to agreement were the 1993 Oslo Accords.

Currently both sides are at loggerheads and the 2002 Roadmap for Peace is in tatters.

A·URAUZE

ISRAEL AND ITS NEIGHBOURS – CAN THEY LIVE TOGETHER?

Israel is a Jewish state isolated in an Arab region. The two sides have historically been at each other's throats – as the wars of 1948, '56, '67 and '73 bear witness. Yet as the conflict matures so have the relationships. *Pocket Issue* looks at the current state of affairs.

Do the Arab countries want peace?

Potentially. Many Arab nations see the settlement of the Palestinian dispute as the starting point of "normal" relations with Israel, as illustrated by the Arab League (King Abdullah) peace plan of 2002 and 2007.

Is this a universal position?

No. There are nations with which Israel now has cordial relations. There are those with which it has a working relationship. Finally, there are those that are still implacably opposed to Israel's place and role in the region.

Israel and its neighbours

GETTING ALONG

Who could be viewed as Israel's "friends" in the region?
Turkey was one of the first countries to establish diplomatic relations with Israel. Since then, only Egypt (in 1979) and Jordan (in 1994, following the Oslo Accords) have fully recognised Israel's right to exist in the region.

Does that mean that all other Middle East nations are hostile?
No. The Gulf States (Bahrain, Kuwait, Oman, Qatar, and the United Arab Emirates) supported a lessening of the Arab boycott of Israel in 1994. Saudi Arabia has recently lifted its ban on

Israeli goods and services as well as driving forward the Arab League's peace proposal.

AT ODDS

What is the "front line" opposition to Israel?
The militant groups – both Islamist and secular – who carry the fight into Israel. The two main ones are Hamas, based in Gaza, and Hezbollah in Lebanon.

Behind these militant groups stand Iran and Syria which play a role in funding and equipping militant organisations and stand accused of fighting a "proxy" war against Israel. Lebanon has often proved the theatre for these wars.

IRAN

Why does Iran oppose Israel?
Israel and Iran are regional powers competing for local influence. Israel is the USA's main strategic ally in the region and Iran is the strongest opponent of American influence.

There is also a religious element. Iran has been an Islamic state

47

since the Revolution of 1979 and therefore stands against the Jewish Israel.

Why is Iran viewed with such concern?

The combination of anti-Israeli rhetoric (current President Mahmoud Ahmadinejad called for Israel to be "wiped from the face of the map" in 2006) and its nuclear ambitions has caused alarm in Israel as well as in the Western world.

Does Iran have nuclear weapons?

Not at the moment but it has an active civil nuclear programme. Many in the West are concerned that the next step will be the development of nuclear weapons. Iran could reach this stage within five years.

How Israel will respond is difficult to say. Though never officially confirmed, it is generally acknowledged that it is the only country that currently has nuclear capability in the region. It is worth remembering that Israel bombed Iraq in 1981 when Iraq threatened to develop nuclear weapons.

Has Iran always been hostile to Israel?

No. Diplomatic ties had been close at times during the Shah's rule, mainly because the USA supported both countries. However, since the Revolution of 1979 Iran has been vehemently hostile towards Israel.

Does Iran support Hamas as well as Hezbollah?

Not formally. They offered financial aid to Hamas following the sanctions imposed by the Quartet after Hamas' 2006 election victory and it is thought that high-level contact exists between them.

SYRIA, LEBANON and HEZBOLLAH

Why are Syria and Israel set against each other?

The Golan Heights (*see map on p16*). Israel annexed this region of Syria during the 1967 war, building Jewish settlements and maintaining a military presence. Syria wants it back.

However, Syria has historically been hostile to Israel and

The Golan Heights is the main point of conflict between Israel and Syria

played a prominent role in the pan-Arab wars of 1948, 1967 and 1973. There was a short "cooling-off" period after the Oslo Accords of 1993, but face-to-face talks came to nothing. It is now thought to be funding both Hezbollah and Hamas.

Why has this conflict centred on Lebanon over the past thirty years?

It goes back to a civil war that started in Lebanon in 1975. The Christian population stood against the Muslim and left-wing factions, the latter supported by the PLO which had moved its base to Lebanon from Jordan in 1970 (following Black September).

Syria and Israel came in on the side of the Christians fearing a wider war and opposing the destabilising activities of the PLO. Both wanted a "friendly"

government in Beirut and opposed the influence of the other in Lebanon.

The Civil War ended in 1990, with Syria helping to broker peace through the Taif Agreement in 1989. Syria kept a military presence in the country until 2005 when its troops were withdrawn following the peaceful Cedar Revolution. Israel, who invaded Lebanon to deal with the PLO, stayed until 2000.

How significant is Hezbollah?

Hezbollah dominates southern Lebanon, virtually forming a state within a state. It is also an important political group, heading up the main opposition to the Lebanese government elected after the withdrawal of Syria in 2005.

Is Hezbollah linked to Hamas?

Not formally. They come from different branches of Islam, Hezbollah is Shia Muslim and Hamas Sunni.

Why does Syria support Hezbollah?

As a way to maintain political

influence in the country as well as to keep pressure on Israel.

Why has there been fighting in the Lebanese refugee camps?
With Lebanon one of the main destinations for Palestinian refugees during the twentieth century, it still has large refugee camps, originally set up for the unskilled. In 2007 the Lebanese army fought with a militant Islamist group, which had formed within the camps.

IRAQ AND THE WAR ON TERROR

Are current events in Iraq linked to the Arab-Israeli conflict?
Not directly. Though there is much debate over the real motives for the US-led invasion of Iraq (see *Pocket Issue, The War on Terror*) the official reason was to deal with Saddam Hussein and his potential threat to Western countries.

Was Saddam anti-Israeli?
Yes, but for political reasons rather than any strong spiritual conviction. Iraq was a secular state under his rule.

How does the new Iraqi government now view Israel?
Despite Saddam's demise, Iraq still holds with its historical position of refusing to recognise Israel's place in the region and its new government is dominated by religious Shia parties.

Are Syria and Iran involved in Iraq too?
Many commentators think that Syria and Iran (both of which border Iraq) are allowing insurgents into the country to fight Allied troops stationed there, and may well be funding and equipping them. The main aim seems to be to prevent the USA from gaining a stable base close to their borders and also to extend their influence in the region.

What other repercussions has Iraq had on the Arab-Israeli conflict?
Iraq's effect on the USA is significant. It is generally thought that the USA is the only effective peace broker in the

Israel-Palestinian dispute. Iraq has diverted both the USA's political energy and will from this question.

The war in Iraq has also affected wider Muslim opinion.

Muslim opinion?

Many Muslims see a double-standard in the willingness of the USA and its allies to invade Iraq yet their unwillingness to put pressure on Israel to address the Palestinian issue. Some argue that this perceived double-standard has increased the threat of attacks by Islamist militants, though governments in Washington and London deny this.

Is Al Qaeda involved in the Israel-Palestinian conflict?

There is no evidence of any formal links between Al Qaeda's leadership and those of Hamas and Hezbollah, and though public overtures have been made to Hamas, they have been rebuffed.

ISRAEL AND ITS NEIGHBOURS – THE ISSUES

From a position of outright hostility in 1948, Arab-Israeli tensions have eased in comparison with the Palestinian conflict.

Egypt and Jordan now have full diplomatic relations with Israel, whilst some other Middle Eastern nations have increased business links.

Outside of the Occupied Territories, Lebanon has been a continued fighting ground for Israel.

Hezbollah is Israel's main enemy within Lebanon.

Many suspect Iran of fighting a "proxy" war in Lebanon through its support of Hezbollah.

The invasion of Iraq has been an important factor for the USA losing focus on the Israel-Palestinian dispute.

PEACE IN THE MIDDLE EAST – WHAT HOPE FOR THE FUTURE?

Many of the problems facing the Middle East seem to be as insoluble as ever. But what are the issues that may shape the future of the region, and is there cause for hope?

What has happened to the Roadmap for Peace?

Its two pillars, that the Palestinian Authority stop the violence and Israel withdraw from the Occupied Territories, are crumbling. Violence continues unabated and although Israel has pulled out of Gaza, settlement has continued in the West Bank.

What are the founders of the Roadmap doing to achieve peace now?

The authors of the Roadmap – the US, the EU, Russia and the UN – are divided in approach. Three factors have undermined their resolve:

Firstly, the election of Hamas in 2006 pulled the rug from under the feet of the PLO, which had been Israel's main "partner for peace".

Secondly, the US-led invasion of Iraq in 2003 diverted political energy and resources, particularly in the US and the UK, to a new problem.

Finally, both Israel and the Palestinians have failed to live up to their commitments as outlined in the Roadmap.

So what now?

The collapse of the Palestinian national unity government in June 2007 has re-focussed international energies on the dispute. Hamas, though holding all the cards in Gaza, has been ousted from government by Mahmoud Abbas, the Fatah leader and Palestinian President. An emergency government has been established and The Quartet and Israel have eased sanctions on his administration.

Can the Palestinian Authority function without Hamas taking a role?

Some commentators now see Abbas as a powerless puppet, too deep in the pockets of the USA and Israel to be considered an effective leader by Palestinians. However recent polls conducted in the Occupied Territories show his popularity to be on the rise and the majority of "ground-level" Hamas supporters favouring dialogue with Israel.

What might be needed?
For peace negotiations to re-start the internal situation in the Palestinian territories needs to be resolved. This is both an issue of leadership and of improving the social and economic lot of the Palestinians within the Occupied Territories.

Leadership?
The USA and Israel are trying to build up President Abbas and his allies to marginalise and, they hope, defeat Hamas. In return, Hamas is trying to present itself as a serious and functioning government for Gaza.

And what could improve the lot of the Palestinians?
A loosening of the Israeli straight-jacket would offer breathing space for the Palestinian economy as would promised, but not delivered, investment from the Gulf States. But the end of factional fighting between Fatah and Hamas, and an end to corruption in the Palestinian Authority, would also help.

Who is the key peace broker?
The USA. A recently leaked UN report admitted that the USA was the only effective power broker for the region. Without its involvement the chances of peace are close to zero.

Is the USA likely to re-engage?
Not whilst it sees the possibility of Hamas, or another Islamist militant party, holding power within the Palestinian Authority. The USA has set itself against the spread of Islamist militancy in the area and the widening of Iranian influence. It is not going to back a Palestinian state led by an Islamist group.

What fuels the USA's concern over Iran?
Iran is anti-American and its influence in the region is growing – in Iraq, Lebanon and in Gaza. Add to this Iran's role in funding militant activity (certainly in the case of Hezbollah and perhaps with Hamas) and its nuclear ambitions.

Israel is worried about being encircled by Iranian influenced states.

What might shape the USA's response?

Events. Three key events with as yet unknown outcomes are on the horizon: The outcome of the 2008 US election and the nature of post-Bush foreign policy. How the war in Iraq develops and how many US resources, for how long, will be directed there. The progress of Iran's nuclear programme.

In the short-term, President Bush has called for a new set of international talks, scheduled for Autumn 2007, to revive the stalling peace process.

PEACE IN THE MIDDLE EAST – THE ISSUES?

The Roadmap for Peace is currently in tatters.

No peace process can move forward until the political situation within the Palestinian territories is resolved.

The USA is the key peace broker.

US policy will be dictated by the behaviour of Iran and whether the US can cut itself free from Iraq.

The Key Players

The people, countries and institutions that will decide the future

THE KEY PLAYERS

Conflict in the Middle East is a global issue that drags in local, regional and global players in the quest for peace. The Key Players takes a look at the people, countries and institutions that are shaping the region.

ISRAEL AND THE PALESTINIAN AUTHORITY

Who currently runs Israel?
Ehud Olmert, though his position is precarious following the unsuccessful campaign in Lebanon in 2006.

Olmert heads up **Kadima** (Hebrew: *forward*), a centre-ground party established in 2005 by **Ariel Sharon** (Prime Minister 2000-06). Kadima won the Israeli election of 2006, breaking the traditional hold on power held by **Likud** and the **Labour Party**. **Shimon Peres**, an old warhorse of Israeli politics and the new Israeli President, left the Labour party to join Kadima.

What happened to Ariel Sharon?
He suffered a stroke in January 2006 that finished his political career. He is still in a coma. **Sharon** was a hugely controversial figure both as a military leader and a politician. It was his visit to the Temple Mount in 2000 that triggered the Second Intifada.

What are Likud and Labour?
Likud (Hebrew: *consolidation*) is the right-wing party who traditionally favour an iron fist in relations with the Palestinians. **Benjamin Netanyahu** (PM from 1996 to 1999) heads up the party. The **Labour** Party, left-of-centre and more in favour of dialogue with the Palestinians, is led by **Ehud Barak** (PM from 1999 to 2001) the ex-soldier who was involved in the failure of the Camp David talks in 2000.

Who holds power in the Palestinian camp?
The two main political groups are **Hamas** and **Fatah**. Fatah holds the presidency of the **Palestinian Authority**, whilst Hamas has a majority in the Parliament. The two sides joined to form a government of

national unity in March 2007 but factional fighting, in which Hamas took control of Gaza, led to its collapse in June 2007. The new Palestinian Prime Minister is **Salam Fayyad**, a liberal politician independent of both Fatah and Hamas.

Who leads Hamas?

Hamas (Arabic: *zeal*), the militant Sunni Muslim group, was originally established in 1987 and is both a political and paramilitary movement. Its political head is **Khaled Mashaal**, based in Damascus following Israeli assassination attempts. **Ismail Haniyeh** was Palestinian Prime Minister until the collapse of the national unity government in June 2007. Hamas now dominates the Gaza Strip.

What about Fatah?

Fatah (Arabic reverse acronym: *Movement for the Liberation of Palestine)* has traditionally been the leading party within the **PLO**. Current leader, **Mahmoud Abbas**, is President of the Palestinian Authority, responsible for dissolving the national unity government with Hamas in June 2007 and

appointing Fayyad as Prime Minister.

Is Fatah an Islamist group?

No, unlike Hamas, Fatah is secular and pro a "two-state" solution to the crisis. However, the group does have militant links, such as the **Al-Aqsa Martyr's Brigades**, who carried out suicide attacks during the Second (Al-Aqsa) Intifada.

Does the PLO still exist?

Yes. It is still viewed as the legitimate voice of the Palestinian people by many Arab nations and represents the Palestinian people within the UN. The **PLO** is an umbrella organisation covering a number of Palestinian groups. Established in 1964 by the Arab League, it was at first violently opposed to the existence of Israel but has since 1988 envisioned a future alongside Israel. **Yasser Arafat** was head of the PLO and Fatah from the late 1960s until his death in 2004. Abbas succeeded him. Hamas is not part of the PLO.

THE NEIGHBOURS

Who stands against Israel in the region?
George W Bush identified (in his words) an "axis of evil" in the area. In addition to Hamas, this included **Hezbollah, Syria, Iran** and Saddam Hussein's **Iraq**.

What is Hezbollah?
Hezbollah (Arabic: *Party of God*) is a political and paramilitary organisation with its power-base in southern Lebanon. It came to prominence after the Israeli invasion of Lebanon in 1982. A Shia Muslim militant group, many countries, including the USA, deem them terrorists, though a number of countries see them as legitimate resistance fighters. Israel invaded Lebanon in 2006 to try and root out Hezbollah's leaders but the campaign was viewed as a failure. The current leader is **Hassan Nasrallah**.

Who runs Lebanon?
Until 2005 Lebanon's politics was dominated by **Syria**, which had played a major role in the country since the Civil War of 1975-90. The assassination, in February 2005, of a former Lebanese PM, **Rafik Hariri**, brought direct Syrian influence to an end. Syria was blamed for his death and the ensuing, peaceful **Cedar Revolution** forced the Syrians to withdraw, bringing about free elections. An anti-Syrian bloc won a majority.

How do Hezbollah and the Lebanese government sit together?
Hezbollah is the largest party of the Shia Muslims and dominates southern Lebanon, though it is not backed by the majority Sunni Muslims, or the Christian parties. It participated in the 2005 elections, winning 10% of the national vote, and is currently trying to block the working of the Lebanese government. Hezbollah receives funding from Syria.

Who runs Syria?
The current president is **Bashar al-Assad**, who took over from his father, **Hafez**, in 2000. Both father and son have led authoritarian regimes that have stood against Israel. Syria was involved in the Arab wars against Israel of 1948, 1967 and 1973.

How does Iran fit into an "axis of evil"?

Iran is an Islamic state suspected of funding Hamas and Hezbollah as well as militants in Iraq. It opposes the right of Israel to exist and Western involvement in the area. The combination of current President **Mahmoud Ahmadinejad's** anti-Israeli rhetoric and Iran's nuclear ambitions is making both the Middle East and the wider world nervous. Supreme leader in Iran is the **Ayatollah Ali Khamenei** and it is he, not Ahmadinejad, who will have the final say in policy.

What about Middle East nations no longer hostile to Israel?

These are led by **Jordan** and **Egypt**. Jordan's King, **Abdullah II**, has followed on from his father, King Hussein, in promoting close ties with Israel (a peace treaty was signed in 1994) and the USA.

Historically, Jordan has been drawn into the conflict due to its border with Israel. It fought Israel in the wars of 1948 and 1967. It also threw out the PLO, who stood accused of fomenting trouble, in the **Black September** war of 1970.

What about Egypt?

Egypt has been ruled by **Hosni Mubarak** since 1981. Mubarak took over from the previous president **Sadat**, after he was assassinated following the 1979 peace treaty with Israel. Mubarak recognises Israel. Egypt is also one of the USA's main allies in the region.

What is Saudi Arabia's position?

Saudi Arabia is one of the dominant forces in the area. The current monarch, **King Abdullah**, has played a major role in developing the Arab League peace proposal of Beirut (2002) and Riyadh (2007).

Saudi Arabia's oil (it has the world's biggest reserves) gives it political and economic clout both in the region and worldwide and it acts as de facto leader of **OPEC**.

What is happening in Iraq?

It is close to civil war. Since the overthrow of **Saddam Hussein** in 2003, it has been dominated by factional fighting between Shia and Sunni groups, as well as militants from beyond its borders. The current Prime Minister, **Nouri al-Maliki**, is struggling to make headway against the insurgents. He has stated that he will not stand for re-election.

Are there other high profile Middle East organisations?
With 22 members the **Arab League** is, at least in principle, the voice of Arab interests for nations in the Middle East and across North Africa.

What about OPEC?
OPEC (Organisation of Petroleum Exporting Countries) is the main power broker in the oil market. OPEC works on a quota system, and aims to maintain a strong, but stable, oil price. It includes members from beyond the Middle East, for example Venezuela which has also been deepening its ties with Iran.

AROUND THE WORLD

Who are the leading peace brokers outside the region?
The 2002 Roadmap for Peace was issued by the "Quartet" – the **USA**, the **EU**, **Russia** and the **UN**.

What is the position of the USA?
The **USA** backs Israel. Even now it gives Israel US$1.2bn in economic aid and US$1.8bn in military aid every year. In comparison (prior to Hamas's election in 2006) the Palestinian Authority received only US$100m in economic aid, though the Palestinian population is a major recipient of humanitarian aid.

What is the policy of the current US administration?
Since 9/11 **George W Bush** has taken a hard line against Iran, Syria, Hamas and Hezbollah. The USA froze financial aid for the Palestinian Authority once Hamas took power. Bush finishes his second term as President in November 2008.

What might happen in the US after 2008?
The two main foreign policy issues in the US are likely to be Iraq and Iran's regional and nuclear ambitions. The leading candidates on both the Democratic and Republican sides have all stated that Hamas' refusal to renounce violence is an obstacle to peace.

What is the policy of the EU?
The **EU** stopped aid to the Palestinian Authority after the election of Hamas but has stated that full support will be given to the newly created emergency Palestinian government based in the West Bank. **Javier Solana** is responsible for the EU's foreign affairs.

What has happened in the UK?
Gordon Brown may address the Middle East with the mindset of an ex-Chancellor. He views economic and social aid as a possible solution to the crisis and may well propose a financial package of support for the area. **Tony Blair** has been nominated as a Middle East envoy to work on behalf of the Quartet.

What is Russia's position?
Russia, under President **Putin**, has adopted a more aggressive stance in the region, criticising US policy and looking to strengthen its influence in a strategically important area. Some see Russia dusting off its old Cold War role in the Middle East. Russia held talks with Hamas after its 2006 election victory and did not support withdrawing aid. It has also sold weapons to **Syria** and states that **Iran's** nuclear ambitions should be "limited" not stopped. Russia is building Iran's nuclear reactor.

And what about the UN?
The secretary general **Ban Ki-moon** is likely to be of peripheral importance when set against American influence. He has recently called for a UN peace keeping force to be sent into the Palestinian territories though there is no agreement on what its mandate would be.

What is the position of the new economic superpower, China?
China, traditionally wary of involving itself in Middle East politics, has recently been developing new ties within the region. It imports oil from **Iran** and **Saudi Arabia** and some argue that Iran's bullish foreign policy has been bolstered by indirect Chinese support. However, China has stated that it does not wish to cut across US "concerns", opposes terrorism and supports the Arab-Israeli peace process.

Stargazing

*What would be a good and bad scenario
come 2020?*

STARGAZING

Conflict in the Middle East and its global repercussions seem to hit the front pages all too frequently. Here we look at how two **possible scenarios** – one good, one bad – may unfold by 2020.

THE GOOD

It is 2020. Israel sits alongside a democratic Palestinian state based in Gaza and the West Bank, with its capital in East Jerusalem. Relations between Israel and the rest of the Middle East, though never completely harmonious, are cordial and business-like.

The turning point? Continued factional fighting between Hamas and Fatah in 2008, and the ensuing media coverage of the plight of the Palestinian people, re-engaged global, and most importantly, American attention.

ISRAEL AND PALESTINE

Hamas and Fatah combine in a national unity government. The army and the police, once central to the factional fighting, exist largely without political interference.

Hamas, isolated following the 2008 fighting and encouraged by post-Bush America's even-handed stance towards Israel, has recognised Israel's right to exist. The USA has taken a watchful, but moderate, stance to Hamas.

The largest settlements in the West Bank are still under Israeli control but many other, smaller settlements have been dismantled. The infamous barrier has also been pulled down.

Israel's withdrawal from East Jerusalem, allowing it to be the capital of the new Palestinian state, allowed Palestinian claims to a "Right of Return" to the lands lost in 1948 and 1967 to be covered by a nominal compensation payment, funded by the USA and the EU.

A productive Palestinian economy based on agriculture and biotechnology, and buoyed by investment from the EU and the Gulf States, has reduced unemployment to less than 10%.

Palestinian society, moderated by years of cultural exchange programmes with Israel and various Western nations, is predominantly Muslim, but legally secular, and held up as a model for moderate Islam and tolerance for the rest of the Middle East.

THE MIDDLE EAST

In the wider world, the success of Palestinian statehood has immeasurably improved Israel's relations with its neighbours, especially Syria and Lebanon.

Iran's nuclear ambitions have, on the outside at least, been limited to civil purposes, though suspicions exist about its ownership of a nuclear weapon. After a period of brinkmanship under President Ahmadinejad, Iran has trodden a more cautious path.

Without Iran providing leadership, Syria and Hezbollah in Lebanon have moderated their stance though both are still keen to limit Israel's influence in the area.

AROUND THE WORLD

With the Palestinian question answered, Iraq's gradual move towards stabilisation and Iran no longer agitating, governments around the world are less concerned about the radicalisation of their Muslim populations. Al Qaeda and other Islamist militants, though still active, now exist on the outreaches of society.

Western dabbling in the Middle East has also been lessened by rapid innovation in the renewable energy markets. Solar, wind and marine power now supply a sizeable chunk of a worldwide energy demand that has also been reduced through greater energy efficiencies. Many cars now run on bio-fuels and the new hydrogen fuel-cell engines. Oil and natural gas no longer hold their central place in the energy mix.

THE BAD

It's 2020. The Fifth Intifada is coming to an end with a death toll of over 1,000 on both the Palestinian and Israeli sides.

Palestinian politics are still dominated by Hamas and other Islamist militants, drawing on the anger caused by Israeli incursions and the poverty within the Gaza Strip and the West Bank.

Attempts to build on the principles of the Oslo Accords and the Roadmap for Peace still continue. The new administration in Washington in 2008 raised hopes for a new settlement, but the outbreak of fighting in 2010 between Hamas, Hezbollah and Israel put paid to that.

ISRAEL AND PALESTINE

An atmosphere of suspicion and mistrust abides. The "cycle of violence" continues with Israeli forces fighting in both Gaza and the West Bank and militants associated with Fatah and Hamas retaliating with provocative rocket launches and suicide bombing missions.

The central leaderships of Hamas and Fatah are virtually powerless to prevent the fighting within the Palestinian Authority and Israel has moved troops back into the Occupied Territories. Israel has also continued to expand the larger settlements in the West Bank.

The economic position of the Palestinians continues to worsen in the Occupied Territories. Poor, and with a bleak future ahead of them, Gaza and the West Bank are now a breeding ground for young militants.

THE MIDDLE EAST

Iran, emboldened by its new range of nuclear weapons, continues to play the spider. It openly funds and equips Hezbollah and Hamas, using them to fight a proxy war against Israel.

The Lebanese government, again heavily influenced by Syria, allows Hezbollah to work as a "state-within-a-state" in southern Lebanon, leading to increased rocket attacks on Israel.

Following the US withdrawal in 2010, Iraq descended into a full-blown civil war with the Shia majority coming out on top. The new Iraqi government aligns itself closely with Iran, forming a dangerous power-bloc.

The US, keen to stem the growth of Islamist militancy in the area, firmly aligns itself with Israel. The region teeters on the brink of a new war, with the added malice of nuclear weapons.

AROUND THE WORLD

Worldwide concern has pushed oil prices over US$140 a barrel. Although global warming and energy security have led governments to diversify their energy sources, Middle East oil and gas is still important and many countries now struggle to sustain their economic growth.

Muslims in western countries have grown alienated from their governments, partly due to the West's failure to alleviate Palestinian suffering. Al-Qaeda remains active with successful attacks on the US embassies in Saudi Arabia, Egypt and the British Embassy in Washington.

In the UK, there has been a continued terror threat coming from disaffected young Muslims. Bomb scares in London are now as common as at the height of the IRA's campaign in the 1970s. The UK government has brought in stringent new laws limiting civil freedom. In the inner cities tension between Muslims and a resurgent British National Party have spilled over into violent riots.

What can you do?

How you can make a mark

WHAT CAN YOU DO?

Ending the conflict in the Middle East is beyond each of us as individuals but there are ways that we can support those striving for peace, by making our voices heard or just helping to make life less uncomfortable for those suffering at the heart of the conflict.

Support a lobbying group

There are a number of political lobbying groups that organise rallies in the UK. One of the biggest is **Enough, www.enoughoccupation.org**, and is supported by a host of celebrities including Emma Thompson, Stephen Fry and Alexei Sayle. It is a coalition of charities, trade unions, faith groups and campaigners.

Jews for Justice, www.jfjfp.org, is another London-based organisation campaigning for justice for Palestinians.

Give generously

In Lebanon there are a number of projects helping Palestinians in Lebanese refugee camps, run by both National and International organisations. A good list of projects can be found on **www.lebanon-support.org**.

Christian Aid, Oxfam and Save the Children all have active projects in Gaza, Lebanon and Israel.

Vote with your wallet

Support the Palestinian economy by buying olive oil and other products locally made. A good list can be found on **www.twinningwithpalestine.net**.

Some organisations in the UK intend to support a boycott of Israeli goods and services. One place to register your opposition is **www.stoptheboycott.org.**

Build bridges

There are many groups in the UK aiming to build bridges between the UK and Palestinians as well as Jews and Palestinians. This could involve a petition or even sending computers from your community to a school in Palestine. Again a good list of

groups is on
www.twinningwithpalestine.net.

The World Council of Churches
also runs an "Ecumenical
Accompaniment Programme"
in Palestine and Israel,
www.eappi.org, with individual
churches twinning with
communities and organising
visits. Ask your local church if
they are running a scheme.

Make some noise

Obviously you can join one of
the campaign groups above
and petition the government
through them. You can also do
your bit to influence the issue.
Cast your vote carefully, based
on each party's commitment
to peace in the Middle East.
Then write a letter to your MP
asking what their policy is and
what he or she is doing about it.

A list of MPs can be found on
www.parliament.org. You can
also sign or start a petition to
10 Downing Street on
http://petitions.pm.gov.uk.
There are petitions supporting
both the Israeli and the
Palestinian positions.

Keep up-to-date

A good starting place for the
latest news is the Middle East
section of the **BBC** News
website, visit
http://news.bbc.co.uk.

Israeli-Palestinian ProCon is
a solid, non-partisan website
discussing the conflict from
both sides. Visit
www.israelipalestinianprocon.org.

One source of pro-Palestinian
news and information is found
at **Electronic Intifada**,
www.electronicintifada.net.
For an Israeli standpoint, visit
the **Haaretz** newspaper
website, **www.haaretz.com**.

The UK's position can be found
on the **Foreign and
Commonwealth Office** website,
www.fco.gov.uk. The **EU**'s
current standpoint is available
on **http://ec.europa.eu**.
For post-Bush foreign policy
in the USA, find out what the
Presidential candidates have
to say at **On the Issues**,
www.ontheissues.org.

The Glossary

Jargon-free explanations

GLOSSARY

A glossary of places, events and organisations that you will have read about in this book or heard in the media.

First Arab-Israeli War (1948)

An Arab coalition – including Iraq, Egypt, Syria, Lebanon, Transjordan (what is now Jordan) – attacked Israel. The main outcomes were that Israel took nearly 80% of the land ear-marked by the UN for a Palestinian state. Egypt took the Gaza Strip, Jordan the West Bank. The Palestinians were left without a homeland.

Al-Aqsa Intifada (2000-05)

Sometimes called the Second Intifada. Uprising in Palestinian territories triggered by Ariel Sharon's visit to the Temple Mount area (that includes the Al-Aqsa Mosque) in Jerusalem in 2000. Wider frustration with a stalling peace process was also blamed, as was the role of Yasser Arafat. Brought to an end in 2005 with Sharm-El-Sheikh truce. Over 1,000 Israelis and 4,000 Palestinians were killed.

Aliyah

Hebrew for "ascent". Used to describe the waves of immigration from Europe into the Palestinian territory from the late 19th century onwards.

Al Qaeda

A Sunni Islamist militant movement headed up by Osama bin Laden. Responsible for the attacks on New York and Washington on the 11th September 2001.

Anti-semitism

Prejudice and hostility towards the Jewish people.

Arab League

A group that coordinates Arab interests for nations in the Middle East and across North Africa. It currently has 22 member nations though is largely thought ineffective when set against national interests.

Balfour Declaration (1917)

A statement issued by then British Foreign Secretary, Arthur Balfour, that recognised the rights of Jews to a homeland in Palestine with the understanding that the rights of the existing Arab population were also recognised. Became embedded in policy once Palestine came under the British Mandate in 1920.

British Mandate (1920-48)

A period of British control of

Palestine, established by the League of Nations, following the collapse of the Ottoman Empire in 1918.

Camp David
Mountain retreat of US Presidents. Location for the 1978 peace accords between Israel and Egypt (that led to the full treaty in 1979) and the failed peace talks between Israel and the Palestinians in 2000.

Cedar Revolution (2005)
Peaceful revolution that pushed Syrian troops out of Lebanon following the assassination of former Lebanese PM, Hariri.

Fatah
Palestinian political party with paramilitary arm that has traditionally dominated the PLO and also the early days of the Palestinian Authority. Yasser Arafat was its leader for many years until his death in 2004. A secular organisation, it backs a two-state solution to the Israeli-Palestinian conflict. Fatah has its power base in the West Bank.

Gaza Strip
One of the Occupied Territories, taken by Israel from Egypt in the 1967 War. After years of maintaining Jewish settlements, Israel withdrew them in 2005. Gaza is dominated by Hamas following the factional fighting of 2007.

Golan Heights
Strategically important Syrian territory occupied by Israel in the 1967 war. The area now contains Jewish settlements and is the main issue of contention between the two sides.

Gulf States
Usually refers to Saudi Arabia, Bahrain, Kuwait, Oman, Qatar, and the United Arab Emirates.

Haganah
A Jewish paramilitary organisation during the period of the British Mandate. Formed the basis of the Israeli army.

Hamas
Palestinian political party with paramilitary arm. A Sunni Islamist militant organisation it is deemed a terrorist organisation by many Western nations. Hamas has its power base in the Gaza Strip.

Hezbollah
Lebanese political party with para-military arm. A Shia Islamic militant movement it is deemed a terrorist organisation by many Western nations. It has its power base in southern Lebanon.

Intifada
Arabic word translated as "uprising". Usually used to refer to the two major uprisings of recent times, the first Intifada (1987-93) and the second, Al Aqsa, Intifada (2000-05).

Kadima
Centre-ground political party founded by Ariel Sharon in 2005. Currently holds power in Israel. Now led by Ehud Olmert following Sharon's stroke in January 2006.

Knesset
The Israeli parliament. Contains a few Arab, as well as Jewish, political parties.

Labour
The major left-wing Israeli political party. Traditionally open to dialogue with the Palestinians.

Likud
The major right-wing Israeli political party. Generally believes in a hard line approach to relations with the Palestinians.

Ma'ale Adumim
Largest Jewish settlement in the West Bank.

Nakba
Arabic word meaning "catastrophe". Usually refers to Israel's founding in 1948 and subsequent dispossession of over 700,000 Palestinian refugees.

Nazi Holocaust
Extermination of the Jews by Germany during the Second World War (1939-45). Estimated that between five and seven million Jews were killed.

Madrid Conference (1991)
Peace talks between Israel and its Arab neighbours set up in wake of Gulf War of 1990-91. Set Israel and the PLO on the path to the Oslo Accords of 1993.

Occupied Territories
Regions occupied by Israel in the 1967 War. Generally refers to the West Bank, East Jerusalem and the Gaza Strip, but also includes the Golan Heights, taken from Syria.

OPEC
The Organisation of Petroleum Exporting Countries. A group of countries that aims to maintain a strong, stable price for oil in the world's markets, without losing customers to alternative energy sources. Members are Saudi Arabia, Iran, Iraq, UAE, Kuwait, Qatar, Algeria, Nigeria, Angola, Libya, Indonesia and Venezuela.

Oslo Accords of 1993

Peace agreement and the high-point of Israeli-Palestinian relations. Palestinians recognised Israel. Palestinian Authority established.

Ottoman Empire

Turkish empire that ruled Palestine (and many other areas) from 15th century until the end of the First World War in 1918.

Palestinian Authority

Interim government established by Oslo Accords of 1993 to govern Palestinian areas in Occupied Territories. Following the factional fighting of 2007 between Hamas and Fatah, the national unity government was dissolved.

The Palestinian Liberation Organisation (PLO)

Group founded by the Arab League in 1964 to represent the Palestinian people. Led from 1969 to 1994 by Yasser Arafat and dominated by his Fatah party. Still the voice of the Palestinian people internationally.

Quartet

The four countries and polities behind 2002's Roadmap for Peace – the UN, USA, Russia and the EU.

Right of return

Can refer to two situations. Firstly, one of the founding elements of the Jewish state is a "right of return" to Israel for every Jew around the world. Secondly, the "right of return" for Palestinians forced from their land in the wars of 1948 and 1967.

Roadmap for Peace (2002)

Peace initiative calling for a Palestinian state side-by-side with Israel, the end of Palestinian aggression and Israel's withdrawal from Occupied Territories.

Sharia Law

Refers to a body of Islamic law, provides a moral code based on the holy books (the Qur'an and the Hadith), centuries of debate and precedence. Provides a legal framework for all aspects of public and private life.

Shia Islam

A branch of Muslim belief. The founding belief is that Mohammed passed succession to his cousin, Ali. The minority group in the Middle East, but with large communities in Iraq, Iran, Lebanon and parts of the Gulf.

Six Day War (1967)

Crushing victory for Israel against an Arab coalition, led by Egypt,

Jordan, and Syria. The main outcome was that Israel began occupation of the West Bank, East Jerusalem and the Gaza Strip (and the Golan Heights), beginning Jewish settlement and sowing the seeds of the current dispute.

Suez Crisis (1956)

Sometimes called the Second Arab-Israeli war. Israel, together with Britain and France, invaded Egypt but lacked support from the USA and were forced to withdraw. The major outcomes were that Israel gained new respect for its military strength, the USA replaced France and Britain as the main influence in the region and Arab nationalism gained momentum.

Sunni Islam

A branch of Muslim belief. The founding belief is that Mohammed passed succession to companion Abu Bakr in the 7th century. 85% of Muslims in the Middle East are Sunni.

Taba Summit (1991)

Summit held in the last days of the Clinton administration between Israel and the Palestinians. Despite initial hopes, it ultimately failed.

Umma

Part of Muslim doctrine. A global Islamic community that surpasses borders, nationality, language, culture or politics. If one Muslim is harmed, the whole community is harmed.

War on Terror

Term coined by George W Bush to describe his response to the 9/11 attacks on the USA.

West Bank

Area occupied by Israel in 1967 War. Named after its location on the west bank of the River Jordan. Population includes 400,000 Jewish settlers.

Yom Kippur War (1973)

An Arab attack on Israel in October 1973 during the Jewish festival of Yom Kippur. Honours roughly even after three weeks of fighting. Broke Israel's aura of invincibility and provided the catalyst for the Egypt-Israel peace treaty of 1979.

Zionist

The Biblical connection between the Jewish people and the land of Israel (Zion is one name for Jerusalem). In the late 19th century, a modern Zionist movement (founded by Theodor Herzl) became a focus for Jewish ambitions. Its core aim was a Jewish state within the borders of Palestine.